Lady Head Vases

Mary Zavada

Photography by Duane Young

Schiffer Publishing Ltd

1469 Morstein Road, West Chester, Pennsylvania 19380

Hey Baby - Found this a few days ago. Decided to wait till I'm "healed" to visit; I'd just be a pain on the road with a broken foot. I'm at the Grand Canyon now. Love CB.

Printed in the United States of America.
ISBN: 0-88740-126-0
Published by Schiffer Publishing Ltd.
1469 Morstein Road, West Chester, Pennsylvania 19380

This book may be purchased from the publisher.
Please include $2.00 postage.
Try your bookstore first.

Front cover: See page 62 for caption.

ACKNOWLEDGMENTS

Bill Locker
Harold Booth
Terry Fish
Harry and Jean Klein
Tommie Zamora
Ellen Anderson
Frank and Betty Cox
Joanne Siefert
W.R. and Louise Allen
Paul and Shirley Dinning
Jeanne Sloan
Carla West
Zofie Fulton
Gloria Young
Jacquelyne North
James Zavada

PREFACE

During the last several years a growing number of people have discovered the joy and pleasure of collecting Lady Head Vases. Hundreds of different vases can be found by the persistent collector to add to a collection. The heads, usually made in a high glaze or soft mat finish semi-porcelain, were produced in Japan and sometimes the U.S.A. They were manufactured from the early 1950's until their decline in popularity in the middle 1960's. From the start, the vases were principally sold to the public by retail florists to hold cut flowers or plants. Starting in 1955, the Irice Co. (Irving W. Rice Co. of New York) also marketed the vases as a gift item containing flower sachet, packaged in net material and tied with a bow. Many of the vase designs were copyrighted and had the date marked on the bottom.

The majority of the vases that can be found are pretty, life-like ladies dressed in the styles of the era. The ladies outfitted with hats, gloves or hair ornaments are quite common. Almost all the ladies can be seen sporting jewelry made of imitation pearls, rhinestones, or fake precious gems. Painted-on gold jewelry was also worn by some of the misses.

Most of the Lady Head Vases had several things in common. They usually displayed only the ladies' shoulders or showed one hand uplifted, often covered by a glove. Generous smiles or open mouths on the vases are a rarity, while a rather blasé or thoughtful expression is the rule. The eyes which come in a variety of colors can be found either open or shut. A few models were made with very realistic brush eyelashes. The hair came in a varied rainbow of hues and elaborate styles were favored. Occasionally a lady was made in more than one size. The sizes ranged from small (under 4½"), medium (4½"-7"), and large (over 7").

Vases in the shape of little girls and babies were also popular. Many of the young girl heads can be found holding things such as animals, flowers, telephones, and umbrellas. Religious theme heads, such as nuns and Madonnas were also made. Many of the pastel-tinted Madonnas were beautifully fashioned and are highly prized by collectors.

The advanced Lady Head Vases collector searches for rarities to add to a growing collection and there are quite a few from which to choose. Vases in the shape of Island girls and Oriental beauties are hard to locate. Very few black ladies, men, or boys were made, so they are normally very difficult to find. A special acquisition for a collector are heads that were made to resemble famous women of the era like Jacqueline Kennedy or have a name on the bottom such as 'Lady Aileen.'

Fortunately the vases were quite often inscribed on the bottom or had a paper label attached. Usually the country of origin, a style number, and/or the name of the distributor is on the vase. Among the many company or brand names that can be found on the vases are:

Alfred J. Weil (Chicago, Ill.)
Ardco (Dallas, Tex.)
Bradley Exclusive
Brinn's (Pittsburgh, Pa.)
Caffco
Chase
Dickson
Enesco
Glamour Girl (U.S.A.)
Inapco
Inarco (Cleveland, Ohio)
Irice (Irving W. Rice Co. of New York, NY)
Lady Head Vase (U.S.A.)
Lee Wards Exclusive
Lefton (Geo. L. Lefton Co.)
Lipper & Mann Creations

M.M.G.
Napco/Napcoware (National Pottery Co. of Cleveland, Ohio)
Norleans
Parma by AAI
Reliable Glassware and Pottery
Relpo (Samson Import Co. of Chicago, Ill.)
Royal Copley
Royal Crown
Royal Sealy
Rubens Originals (Los Angeles, Cal.)
Shawnee (U.S.A.)
Sonsco
Stanfordware (Sterling, Ohio)
Tilso
Trimont Ware
Ucago (United China & Glass Co. New Orleans, La.)
Uoagcochina
Vcagco Ceramics
Velco (Los Angeles, Cal.)
Victoria Ceramics
Vimax Creation
Wales

A lovely brown-haired lady with an uplifted hand wears a black and white dress, with pearl earrings and a matching necklace. Marked Brinn's, Pittsburgh, Pa, made in Japan, TP-1821. (7½")

A young, sweet-faced blonde beauty wears an old fashioned bonnet which ties under her chin. The bonnet is trimmed with flowers and gold glitter. Marked Lipper & Mann Creations, Japan. (5¾")

Left: Freckle-faced, white-haired country miss wears a green straw hat and pearl necklace. Marked Sonsco, Japan. (5")

Middle: Demure blonde lady wears pearl earrings and a black dress. Her hair and dress are decorated with white and gold flowers with pearl centers. Marked E2188. (6")

Right: A pretty lady with arched brows and white hair trimmed with gold wears a white glove and ring on her uplifted hand. She also wears a pearl necklace. No marks. (5½")

Left: Lively, brown-haired lass wears a smart green hat. She is also wearing matching pearl earrings and necklace. Marked Parma by AAI, Japan, 220. (5½″)

Middle Cute, young, blonde with a very slender neck wears a blue dress and blue flowers in her hair. Marked Parma by AAI, Japan, A-222. (5¼″)

Right: Lady with up-turned brown hair decorated with a butterfly is wearing basic black and pearls. Marked Parma by AAI, Japan, A-172. (5½″)

Left: Sophisticated blonde lady wears a black dress and a white hat trimmed in gold. Her uplifted hand sports a gold bracelet set with rhinestones. Marked Napco, Japan, 1958, 63282. (5½")

Middle: Wide-eyed belle is wearing a black dress with white collar. A perky black bow graces her hair. Long, dangly pearl earrings and matching necklace complete her outfit. Marked Napcoware, Japan, C8499. (5½")

Right: A white and gold hat adorns the blonde hair of a worldly lady. Her low cut black dress is decorated with a white and gold broach. A white glove encases her uplifted hand. Her outfit is completed with fancy pearl earrings and necklace. No marks. (5")

Left: With her chin resting on her uplifted hand this chic lady with downcast eyes displays a white hat trimmed with gold dots, yellow ribbon and flowers. No marks. (5½")

Middle: A brown haired lady with a charming face wears a bow-trimmed dress and pearl jewelry. Marked Parma by AAI, Japan, A173.(5¼")

Right: Handsome woman with white hair trimmed in gold wears a yellow dress, gold broach, and long pearl earrings. Marked Wales, made in Japan. (5½")

13

Left: Upswept brown hair and downcast eyes mark this elegant lady who wears a white dress trimmed in gold. Pearl jewelry complete the outfit. Mark Inarco, Japan, Cleveland, Ohio, 1963, E1067 (7")

Middle: A pretty, young girl with her hair in ringlets wears a yellow dress trimmed in white ruffles and black ribbon. A yellow hat with black bow complete her ensemble. No marks. (6")

Right: A refined lady with blonde hair is wearing a black dress adorned with a white ruffle and pearl jewelry. Marked Rubens Originals Los Angeles, Japan, 4123. (6¾")

Left: Comely lady with blonde hair wears basic black and pearls. Marked Napcoware Cleveland, Ohio, made in Japan, c7293 (5½")

Middle: Wearing a green dress, this handsome lady has reddish brown hair decorated with a bow. Marked Japan.(5½")

Right: A black dress and pearl jewelry are worn by this elegant blonde lady. Marked Parma by AAl, made in Japan, A-108. (5½")

Left: Wearing a matching pink hat and dress, this charming lady rests her chin against her uplifted hand. Marked Tilso, hand-painted, Japan. (5¾")

Middle: With her chin resting on the thumb of her uplifted hand, this attractive lady is dressed in purple. Marked Rubens Originals Los Angeles, Japan, 482. (5")

Right: Personable blonde lady with downcast eyes wears a green dress trimmed in gold and a green hat with brown ribbon. Marked Lee Wards Exclusive, Japan. (5")

Left: A wreath of blue flowers embellishes the blonde hair of this graceful lady dressed in white. Marked Napco, Hand-painted, Japan, © 1962, C5676. (6¼")

Middle: Wearing a black glove on her uplifted hand, this fine lady is adorned with a white and gold ornament in her hair and a ribbon around her neck. Marked Japan. (5¾")

Right: Refined lady with arched eyebrows wears a black hat decorated with white and gold roses. The hat matches the black dress with white and gold trim. Marked Relpo, K1053A. (5¾")

Left: Hard-to-find Lady with her gray hair dressed in ringlets and decorated with white and gold flowers wears a black ribbon around her throat. No marks. (6″)

Right: This enchanting angel with flowing hair and hands crossed upon her breast is also hard-to-find. Marked Napco, © 1956, C2912B. (5¾″)

Left: Dainty brown-haired lady wears a bright red ruffled dress, matching white and gold broach and earrings, and pearl necklace. No marks. (3½")

Middle: A charming blonde lady wears a white hat trimmed with a purple flower and a blue dress. No marks. (5¾")

Right: Perky lady with pink flowers tucked behind her ear wears a pink dress and pearl jewelry. Marked Caffco, Made in Japan, E-3292 (4½")

Left: Delicate blonde woman with pearl jewelry is dressed in a pink and white dress with matching hat. Marked Vcagco Ceramics Japan. (5½″)

Middle Brown-haired beauty with downcast eyes is very chic in a green hooded garment trimmed with purple flowers. Marked Wales, made in Japan (5¾″)

Right: Aloof lady with chin in the air and uplifted hand touching her face wears matching pearl jewelry, white and gold hat and simple black dress. Marked Napco, © 1956, C2636A. (6¼″)

Left: Comely lady with a white and gold flower in her brown hair wears a black dress and pearl jewelry. Marked Ardco, Fine Quality, Dallas, made in Japan. (5½")

Middle: Lively blonde maiden wears a black hat enhanced with a white and gold ribbon which ties under her chin. Marked Relpo Chicago, Ill, Japan, 2031. (5½")

Right: With bows in her blonde hair, this charming girl wears a white, yellow and black dress. Marked Relpo Chicago, Ill. Japan, 2031. (5½")

Left: Large lady with an amiable face wears a green and white dress with a white collar. Marked Relpo, 2188. (7″)

Middle: An uplifted hand touches the cheek of this brown-haired lady wearing a print dress with white ruffled collar. Marked Relpo, © Samson Import Co. 1964, Japan, 5543A. (6″)

Right: A white-gloved hand touches the face of this brown-haired damsel wearing an orange dress with matching beret. Marked Relpo, made in Japan, K169415. (5½″)

Left: With a flower in her brown hair, this little girl wears a blue dress. Marked Inarco. Japan, E-3157. (5½″)

Middle: Little girl with her hair covered by a pink scarf decorated with white and yellow daises. No marks. (6″)

Right: Sweet faced little girl wearing a blue jumper, white sweater, and a blue ribbon in her brown hair. Marked Inarco, E-2767. (5½″)

Left: Lovely, brown-haired damsel wears a white and gold hat with a green ribbon and pearl earrings. Marked Relpo, K1517. (5¾″)
Middle: A ring enhances the uplifted hand of this elegant brown-haired belle. Marked Trimont Ware, Japan. (6¾″)
Right: Attractive blonde miss wears a flower in her hair and basic black with pearls. Marked Relpo, K2067. (5½″)

Left: Rare Island girl wears a green sarong and a hibiscus in her black hair. Marked Shawnee, U.S.A., 896. (6")

Middle: Lively young lass with her hair in pig tails wears a green dress and matching head scarf. Marked Inarco, E2523. (5¾")

Right: Rare, bare-breasted Island girl wears flowers in her long black hair. No marks. (5¾")

Left: A lovely young lady with her brown tresses tied with a black ribbon is wearing a black dress with white collar and pearl jewelry. No marks. (5½")

Middle: With a white and gold glove covering her hand, this refined woman is wearing a black dress, pearl jewelry, and a black hat trimmed with a white and gold ribbon. Marked Inarco, C-2322. (7")

Right: With an uplifted hand touching her cheek, this unusual auburn-haired lady is wearing pearl jewelry, a V-necked pink dress, and a rose in her hair. Marked Inarco Cleveland, Ohio, 1962, E-779. (6")

Left: This charming maiden is wearing a white and gold hat trimmed with blue roses, and a black and green dress decorated with a white bow with gold dots. Marked Ardco, Fine Quality Dallas, made Japan. (5¾")

Middle: With her chin resting on her uplifted hand, this lanquid blonde is wearing pearl jewelry and a matching hat and dress. Marked Inarco, 1961, E190/L. (6¾")

Right: Auburn-haired damsel with her fingers touching her chin is wearing pearl earrings, white hat embellished with pastel flowers, and a pink and white dress. Marked Vimax Creation, Japan. (5¼")

Left: Lady with her hair cut in bangs is wearing a dress with a lace jabot. Marked Relpo, Japan, K1817. (5¾")

Middle: Beautiful, youthful maiden with long blonde hair decorated with purple bows is wearing a purple and white dress and pearl earrings. Marked Relpo, 2004. (7")

Right: Large green bows enhance the brown hair of this lady wearing a dark green dress with white ruff. Marked Relpo, Chicago, Ill., Japan, K1663. (5¾")

Left: Blonde lady head vase which looks remarkably like Princess Diana of England. Marked Ardco, fine quality, Dallas, Japan, C3253. (5½")
Middle: Handsome lady is wearing a green dress, a matching bow in her brown hair, and pearl jewelry. Marked Relpo, Japan, K1696. (5½")
Right: Flirtatious miss with her hands under her chin is wearing a gray dress, matching hat with white and black ribbon, and pearl earrings. Marked Relpo, K1175/s. (5")

Left: A black hat trimmed with white and gold ribbon and green plume is perched on the blonde hair of this lady wearing a black dress with white and gold collar. Marked Inarco, Japan, © 1961, E-191/m/b. (5½")

Middle: Languid brown-haired lady with her hand brushing her cheek is wearing a black dress and pearl jewelry. Marked A174. (7")

Right: With her hand almost touching her lips, this elegant lady with her hair in ringlets wears a black dress with white and gold ruffle and matching hat. Marked Made in Japan, C6016. (5½")

Two sizes of the same lady head vase with upswept blonde hair decorated with gold painted on tiarras set with fake red jewels. Marked Lefton, Japan. (4¼", 8")

Pair of charming maidens with the blonde in a ruffled dress with the matching bonnet trimmed in blue ribbon and the brunette in the same outfit with pink ribbon. Marked Norleans, Japan. (7½")

Left: Cute, red-cheeked baby in ruffled bonnet. No marks (5¾")
Middle: Full figure, naked kewpie vase. Marked Lefton, Japan, 3631 (7")
Right: Blue eyed, blonde, baby in a pink blanket. Marked E-4091. (5")

Left: Lovely lady dressed in yellow with a matching hat clutches a purse in one white gloved hand while the other smooths her hair. A painted on gold necklace set with a fake red jewel completes her ensemble. Marked 1736. (5½")

Middle: White lady detailed in gold in a high glaze finish wears a pink dress ornamented with a yellow rosebud with matching hat. Marked Lefton's, Japan, PY641. (5¾")

Right: A pink hat trimmed with a white ribbon matches the dress worn by this red-haired belle. Marked Lefton, Japan, 3130. (4½")

Left: This comely, black haired damsel is looking upward while she rests her arm. She is wearing a garden party hat and dress with matching flower print. Marked Lefton's, Japan, /343r. (5¾")

Middle: Elegant, blonde lady has one white-gloved hand raised while the other crosses her bosom. She is wearing a strapless gown, pink shawl, and white and pink hat. Marked Lefton's, Japan. (6")

Right: Supercilious blonde wears a lustre finish white gown, glove and hat. A pearl necklace adds the finishing touch. Marked Lefton's, Japan, 3278. (5¾")

Left: This chic, black-haired lady with her chin propped on her black gloved hand is wearing a black and gold dress with matching neck ribbon. A white and gold hat trimmed with black completes her costume. Marked © Geo. L. Lefton, w50506. (5¼")

Middle: Stylized woman with white hair touched with gold is attired in white, pink, and gold. Marked Lefton's, Japan. (6")

Right: Brown haired lass with a lively look in her eyes is arrayed in a matching dress and hat. White and gold flower earrings put the finishing touch on her finery. Marked © Geo. L. Lefton 1957, 162B. (5½")

Left: Modest blonde maiden with downcast eyes is clad in a white and gold dress with matching hat. The hat is adorned with a pink ribbon which trails to her shoulder. Marked Japan. (4¾")

Middle: Good-looking, brown-haired, lady wears a matching pink hat and dress. She sports painted-on earrings. Marked Japan. (6½")

Right: Sweet-faced, old fashioned girl is modestly attired in a pink bonnet and dress. The dress is trimmed in gold glitter. Marked Japan. (6")

Three young girls carrying umbrellas to match their ensembles. The umbrella and handle are made of china and the stick of metal.
Left: Marked Vcagco, Japan. (8¼")
Middle: Marked Japan. (7")
Right: marked 52/256 (8")

38

Left: Pretty blonde with downcast eyes and raised hand is outfitted in a nurse's uniform and cap. No marks. (5¼")

Middle: Beautiful brown-haired miss is dressed for Christmas. She is wearing a red dress trimmed in white and gold. Her hat is garnished with holly. Marked x7638 Napco, 1962. (5½")

Right: Rare, spectacle clad, lady head vase. The lady has her brown hair in pigtails and is holding a vase of flowers. No marks. (5½")

Three cute, pigtailed, young girls are carrying umbrellas. All three are marked Japan. Many times the mark is found on the umbrella. (8½″, 8¾″, 6¾″)

Left: Young, brown haired, cowboy dressed in yellow hat and kerchief with a star on his chest. Rare. No marks. (6")

Middle: Boy Graduate in cap and gown, clutching a diploma in his hand. Marked Napco, 1959, c4072A. (5¾")

Right: Hard-to-find girl graduate in pink, tasseled cap and gown. No marks. (5")

Left: Winking blonde lass is outfitted in a pink dress ornamented with pink ribbon. Her blue hat is trimmed with pink roses. No marks. (5¼")

Middle: Fashionable young lady is dressed in Carnaby street mod style. Her getup includes a green turtleneck sweater and brown cap. No marks. (6½")

Right: Adolescent blonde has her hair in braids which are ornamented with pink bows that match her dress. No marks. (5¾")

Three enchanting ladies with upswept blonde hair are costumed in Elizabethan inspired gowns. Hard-to-find. No marks. (6¼", 6½", 6¼")

Left: Auburn-haired lady with a pleasant face is dressed in pink and wears pink flower shaped earrings. No mark. (4")

Middle: Winsome youngster with white hair is wearing a blue hat and matching dress ornamented with white collar and pink rosebud touched with gold. Marked Chase, Hand-painted, made in Japan. (4½")

Right: Shy looking, pleasant-faced lady is wearing a blue dress and blue flower earrings. No marks (4")

Left: A young girl with her blonde hair tied with a ribbon holds a bouquet of flowers in her hands. She is dressed in blue, Marked Enesco, Japan. (6")

Middle: Red-haired girl is wearing a hat trimmed with pink ribbon which ties under her chin. She holds a white poodle in her hands. Marked Japan. (6¼")

Right: A young girl with brown hair wearing pink holds a bouquet of flowers clutched in her hands. She is very similar to the blonde girl in this picture. Marked Enesco, Japan. (6")

Left: This pretty, happy youngster has her brown hair in a ponytail and is wearing a green dress. A ring decorates her hand. Marked Napcoware, c5037. (6″)

Middle: Winsome, blonde, urchin in pink, holds a white kitten cuddled in her hands. She has a white ribbon with red polkadots in her hair. No marks. (¾″)

Right: Dressed in black with her brown hair in pigtails, this sweet girl holds a yellow rose in her hand. Marked Made in Japan, c6049. (5½″)

Rare trio of goldskinned beauties wear fancy white and gold trimmed head dresses. Each wears a set of pearl earrings. All three are marked Royal Sealy, Japan. (5¾", 5½", 5¾")

Left: A brown-haired miss has her tresses embellished with a black ribbon. She is wearing a white sleeveless frock trimmed in black. Marked Royal Crown, 3470, Handpainted. (4½")
Middle: Blonde adolescent has her hair in ponytails and is wearing a sleeveless, ruffled, white dress trimmed with a pink band and black flowers. No marks. (5½")
Right: Blonde lady with downcast eyes and a reserved expression is rigged out in black and white striped dress. Marked Royal Crown, handpainted, 3470. (4¾")

46

Left: Smiling, brown-haired adolescent is dressed in white. She is holding a blue telephone to her ear. No marks. (4¾")

Middle: Gorgeous belle with her hair fixed in ringlets is arrayed in a green dress and a double strand of pearls. Green and white blossoms bedeck her couiffure. No marks. (5½")

Right: Wide-eyed maiden is dressed in white trimmed with gold. Green and white flowers enhance her red hair. Marked 7303. (5½")

Left: Brown haired damsel with a delicate face is outfitted in a lavender sweater with a white-ribbed collar and matching beret. A gold broach adorns her collar. Marked Inarco, Japan. (5¾")

Middle: Large, blasé, brown-haired lady has her head tilted and her hand uplifted. She wears a green dress and matching pearl jewelry. Nomarks. (7½")

Right: This brown-haired woman is attired in a light blue frock trimmed in navy with a matching navy blue hat garnished with a light blue bow. She is wearing pearl jewelry. Marked Napcoware, c7494. (5¾")

Left: Modest lady with white hair touched with gold is clad in a yellow dress. A yellow hat with a large pink ribbon tied under her chin completes her outfit. No marks. (5¼")

Middle: Unusual lady with reddish brown hair and oriental looking eyes is wearing a religious necklace. Her dress is green and white with a matching hat. On the bottom, in red fingernail polish, is written the date, 1957. Marked Japan. (7")

Right: Smug, white matron trimmed in gold sports a painted on gold necklace. She wears a yellow gown and matching yellow hat trimmed with a pink rosebud. Marked Handpainted, Made in Japan. (6½")

Right: Brown-haired young lass with downcast eyes wears a green and blue dress and rhinestone earrings. Marked Velco, L.A. Calif., Japan, 6689. (5¾")

Middle: Charming, wide-eyed, urchin with red hair is holding two valentines. She is wearing a white dress and a white hat trimmed in pink. Marked Velco, L.A. Calif., Japan, 11190. (6")

Right: Brown-haired girl with downcast eyes is wearing a blue jumper and white blouse. A flower printed scarf covers her hair. Marked Velco, L.A. Calif., Japan, 6686. (5½")

Left: Brown-haired woman wearing a brown and white hat and dress has her chin resting on her hand. She is wearing pearl jewelry and blue eye shadow. Marked Rubens Originals, Japan, 476. (5")

Middle: Comely belle has her blonde hair fixed in layered bangs and braids. She wears a high collared dress, pearl earrings, and a flower in her hair. Marked Rubens Originals, Japan, 4135. (5½")

Right: Dainty blonde miss wears a blue dress decorated with purple flowers, matching hat, and pearl earrings. Marked Rubens Originals, Japan, 498. (4¾")

Left: Blue-eyed miss with brown hair is wearing a green hat and white dress. Marked Enesco, Japan. (7")

Middle: Attractive lady with uplifted hand is wearing a green dress with white flowered collar and pearl jewelry. Marked Enesco Japan. (7")

Right: Handsome lady with brown hair piled loosely on top of her head and tied with a blue ribbon, is wearing a pink dress and pearl earrings. Marked Enesco, Japan. (7½")

Left: Pretty lady with downcast eyes is wearing a black dress ornamented with two white flowers trimmed in gold and pearl jewelry. Marked Ardco, Dallas, made in Japan. (5¾″)

Middle: Exquisite blonde miss with downcast eyes is wearing a white glove, white hat, pearl necklace, and a black dress with white collar. Marked Napco, made in Japan, C5047. (6½″)

Right: Personable lady with downcast eyes has a white and gold bow in her brown hair. She is clad in a black gown with white and gold collar. Marked Ardco, Dallas, made in Japan. (6″)

Left: Aloof blonde belle with downcast eyes is wearing a brown frock lined in white, pearl earrings, and a brown and white hat. Marked Napco, © 1959, C38158. (5¾")

Middle: Languid lady with downcast eyes is wearing a black glove, pink dress, and white hat trimmed with two flowers. Marked Napco, 1960, C50358. (5¾")

Right: Reserved, brown-haired woman has her uplifted hand touching her face. She is attired in a blue gown, pearl jewelry, and a blue hat trimmed in gold and white. Marked Napco, © 1956, C3307c. (5¾")

Left: Young, lovely blonde girl is praying. She is dressed in a red gown. Rare. Marked © Inarco, Cleve. Ohio, 1962, E-776. (5¼")

Middle: Cute, blue-eyed tot is dressed in a frilly pink gown with a pink bow in its hair. Marked Inarco, Japan, E-3156. (5½")

Right: Young praying boy with reddish brown hair is dressed in blue. Rare. Marked Inarco, Japan, E-1579. (5¾")

Left: Pretty damsel with her long brown hair tied with a black bow is garbed in a black dress with white buttons. Marked Japan. (5½")

Middle: Lady with her white and brown hair tied in ponytails is wearing pearl jewelry and a mustard yellow dress with a high white collar. Marked Rubens originals, Los Angeles, made in Japan, 4123. (5¾")

Right: Beautiful maiden is wearing a black gown and has pink flowers embellishing her long blonde hair. Marked Rubens, Japan, 4136. (5½")

Left: Meek miss has brown hair tied with black bands. She is wearing a yellow dress with a white and gold ruffled collar. Marked Rubens, Japan, 4125. (4½")

Middle: Brown-haired lady with downcast eyes is wearing a simple blue dress. Marked Rubens, Japan, 4125. (4¼")

Right: Shy lady has her brown hair decorated with two white and gold flowers with pearl centers. She is wearing a pale green dress with white and gold collar. Marked Enesco, Japan. (4½")

Pretty lady with head slightly tilted and eyes looking up, has a black gloved hand touching her cheek. Her ensemble includes a white dress trimmed in gold, a pink and gold broach, pearl necklace and black hat. Marked C1963, Rubens, La. Calif. 487m. (6¼")

Lady with her blonde hair pinned up is dressed for riding. She wears a tophat and has a gold and white broach with a picture of a horse on her habit. Rare. Marked Rubens, Japan, 530. (6")

Left: Lady with her brown hair fixed in soft curls is wearing a pearly pink sleeveless dress, pearl earrings, and pink hair bow. Marked Enesco, Japan. (5½")

Middle: Thoughtful woman taps her face with her hand. Her finery includes pink hair bow, pearl earrings, and white and gold gown. Marked Rubens, Japan, 489. (6½")

Right: Lady with her blonde hair decorated with a black bow wears a black dress trimmed in white. Marked Enesco, Japan. (5½")

Sultry belle is holding the brim of her straw picture hat in her uplifted hand. She is garbed in a white and gold gown. Marked Napco, © 1956, C2632B. (7¼″)

Striking black woman is wearing a yellow turban, red dress, three strand necklace, and gold hoop earrings. Black lady head vases are very rare. Marked Japan. (5″)

Left: Small, blonde christmas girl is wearing a red coat, white muffler decorated with holly, and white and gold hat. Marked Inarco, Cleve, Ohio, E-1274. (3¾")

Middle: Small boy dressed in a fireman's helmet and black coat is holding a red and gold water hose in his hands. Marked Inarco, Japan. (5¼")

Right: Lady with downcast eyes is wearing a Santa Claus hat trimmed with a poinsettia. Around her neck is a red scarf with white polka dots. Marked © Napco, Handpainted, 1962, cx5409. (5")

Left: Blonde child with downcast eyes is wearing a blue white, and gold dress ornamented with a pink rose. Her white hat is trimmed with black ribbon and a rose. Marked 7304. (5″)

Middle: Restrained lady with brown hair is wearing a white dress trimmed in black and gold. The white and black hat she is wearing is adorned with two large blue and yellow flowers. Marked Relpo, K860. (6″)

Right: Smiling blonde girl with her hair in braids, is wearing a blue dress with a white collar edged in black. Marked Inarco, Japan. (5″)

Left: Blue-eyed blonde miss wears a black ribbon, pearl earrings, and a white dress trimmed in black. Her bright pink lipstick is very unusual since the vast majority of lady head vases have red lips. Marked Enesco, Japan. (5½″)

Middle: A pink and white head scarf is covering the brown hair of this lady with downcast eyes. Marked Enesco, Japan. (5½″)

Right: Lovely blonde lady has her hair fixed in soft curls and long bangs. Her outfit includes pearl jewelry, and a sleeveless white dress trimmed in black. Marked Enesco, Japan. (5½″)

Left: Refined blonde with downswept eyes wears a white glove, a black dress with white collar, pearl jewelry, and a white hat trimmed in black. Marked Napcoware, C 5046. (4½")

Middle: Beguiling brown-haired woman with downcast eyes is attired in a peach dress with white collar, pearl earrings, and peach hat trimmed with white ribbon and long plumes. Marked Inarco, © 1961, E-191/m/c, (5½")

Right: Attractive brown haired damsel wears a green and gold ring upon her hand and an unusual pink and white hooded garment. Marked Inarco, Cleve, Ohio, E-2005. (4½")

Left: Pretty lady with her brown hair fixed in a page boy style has her uplifted hand near her cheek. Her ensemble includes a white hair bow, pearl necklace, and pink dress with scalloped neckline. Marked Inarco, Cleve, Ohio, 1964, Japan, E-2005. (4¾")

Middle: Cosmopolitan belle has her hand resting against her face. Her green gown is festooned with rhinestones and her white hat with green and black stripes is garnished with a white and gold ribbon. Marked Napco © 1956, C1775A. (7¼")

Right: Brown-haired woman is wearing pearl earrings and a pastel green dress ornamented with a white and gold bow on one shoulder. Marked Enesco, Japan. (4½")

Adorable young girl with brown hair is attired in her Sunday best pink gown decorated with large white bow with maroon and green stripes. A pink rose adorns her matching hat. Marked Napco, 1956, C1838B. (5¾")

Captivating Lady Aileen with downcast eyes and blonde upswept hair is all rigged out for an evening on the town. Her finery includes a basic black dress, a painted-on gold tiara set with fake green jewels and a matching necklace. Marked Inarco, Cleve, Ohio, Lady Aileen, © 1964, E-1756. (5¾")

Left: Attractive woman is wearing a pearl necklace and a white dress with scalloped neckline and bow trimmed in gold. Marked Napco, © 1962, Hand Painted, Japan, C5675. (6″)

Middle: Engaging blonde beauty is clad in a white dress touched with gold, matching hat, and pearl jewelry. There is a white glove and painted-on gold bracelet on her upraised arm. Marked Inarco, © 1961, Cleve, Ohio, Japan, E-241. (6½″)

Right: Aloof brown-haired lady is wearing a black dress, pearl jewelry, and a gold hair ornament. Marked Inarco, Japan, E1062. (6″)

Left: Graceful lady with her hand tapping her cheek wears a pink rose in her blonde hair. She is attired in a pale pink dress and pearl jewelry. Marked Inarco, © 1961, Japan E 193/m/b. (5¾")

Middle: This brown-haired miss has her eyes closed and her head slightly tilted. She is wearing a sleeveless black dress, white and gold broach, and pearl jewelry. Marked Enesco, Japan. (5½")

Right: Restrained blonde maiden with slightly tilted face is wearing a ruffled white dress touched with gold, gold broach, and pearl jewelry. Marked Napcoware, C5939. (6")

Left: Brown-haired belle with a personable face is wearing a green jumper, a white blouse ornamented in gold, and a green hat with pink and blue flowers that ties under the chin. Marked Velco, Japan, 3748. (5½")

Middle: Good-looking lady with downcast eyes and upswept brown hair needs to have her paint retouched. She is wearing pearl jewelry, a blue dress, and a matching hair band. Marked Rubens, Japan, 485. (6½")

Right: Enchanting damsel with long blonde hair is wearing a green dress with ruffle and white collar, pearl earrings, and a yellow hat trimmed with a white bow with gold dots. Marked Vcagco, Japan. (5½")

Left: Demure lass with downcast eyes and one hand touching her face has her long blonde hair tied in a ponytail. She is wearing pearl earrings, a white and gold ruffled dress and matching hairbow. Marked Velco, Japan, 3688. (5½")

Middle: Brown-haired lady is wearing pearl jewelry, a green dress with white collar trimmed in gold and a matching green hat. Marked Inarco, Cleve, Ohio, Japan, © 1963, E-969/s. (4½")

Right: Modest lady with short grey hair is wearing pearl earrings, white dress edged in gold, and a large red flower corsage on her shoulder. Marked Vcagco, Japan. (6")

Left: Lady has a blue hat trimmed with white and gold roses perched on her blonde hair. She is wearing pearl earrings and a black dress banded in white and dotted with gold. Marked M.M.G., Japan. (4½″)

Middle: Sleepy looking woman with her chin propped on her entwined fingers is wearing white gloves, pearl jewelry, brown dress with white collar, flower brooch, and white hat. Marked Rubens, Japan, 495. (5¾″)

Right: Brown-haired lady with downcast eyes is wearing a blue dress with white collar and matching hat trimmed with a white and pink bow. Marked Napco, © 1958, C3342c. (4½″)

Three cute children wearing hats, made by Royal Copley, could be used as vases or wall pockets. The flattened backs have a hole drilled in them. Marked Royal Copley. (7", 6½", 7")

Left: Tanned lady with white hair is wearing an old fashioned, yellow bonnet and a low cut, yellow ruffled dress. Marked H (7¾")

Right: Timid maiden named Ginger with downcast eyes and tilted face is wearing an orange bonnet trimmed in white and a matching coat ornamented with pink flowers. Marked Lefton's, Japan, Ginger. (6¼")

Left: Adorable baby with a winsome smile dressed in white with gold trimming could be used as a vase or wall pocket. No mark. (5¼″)
Right: Young girl, with her brown hair tied in ponytails, is wearing a blue straw hat decorated with a white ribbon with tiny red flowers and a white dress with red flowers. She could be used as a wall pocket or vase. Marked Brinn's, Pittsburgh, Pa., made in Japan, TV-1473. (5¼″)

Three different vases that could also be used as wall pockets. The little girl holding a doll is marked U.S.A., 810. The two ladies dressed in blue and maroon were made by Royal Copley. (6½", 6", 6")

Striking lady has her blonde hair fixed in a page boy style with long bangs and curls on top of her head. She is wearing a black dress and pearl earrings. Marked Enesco, Japan. (5¾")

Rare character head of a mournful Jacqueline Kennedy in her widow's weeds. Marked Inarco, Cleve Ohio, © 1964, E-1852. (6")

76

Left: Petite, blonde, belle is wearing a white ruffled gown highlighted in gold, a gold broach, and pearl earrings. Marked National Potteries, Bedford, Ohio. CF6060. (3½")

Middle: Lady with downcast eyes and tilted head wears a simple dress, hat, and glove in lustre white. Marked 1115. (5½")

Right: Charming young girl with blonde hair wears a white hat decorated with two red poinsettias and a white dress with gold drawstring. Marked Inarco, Cleve, Ohio, Japan, 1964, E1247. (3¾")

Left: Adorable little girl with rosy cheeks has white hair touched with gold and is wearing a white dress trimmed with gold. Marked Japan. (5½")

Middle: Sleeping young tot is yawning. She is wearing a white cap and gown embellished with gold. Marked Ucago, Hand painted, Japan. (5¼")

Right: Cute little boy with white hair touched with gold is the companion piece to the girl on the far left of the picture. He is wearing a white suit trimmed in gold and a ruffled cravat. Marked Japan. (5¾")

Left: Pale lady with downcast eyes and unusual pink hair is wearing a white hat, white dress, pearl necklace, and pink flower earrings with pearl drops. No marks. (3½")

Middle: Short haired lady with head slightly tilted is wearing a white glove on her uplifted hand, white dress, matching hat, and pearl jewelry. Marked Victoria Ceramics, Made in Japan. (5¼")

Right: Brownhaired maiden with downcast eyes is wearing a pink and white beret and blue flowered earrings with pearl drops. Marked Japan. (3½")

Three similar lady head vases are all decorated differently. *Left:* Marked Glamour Girl, U.S.A. (6¼") *Middle:* No marks. (6¼") *Right:* Marked Lady Head Vase, U.S.A., 11B. (5")

Two lady head vases with blonde hair have long painted-on eyelashes. No marks. (7½" to 5")

Left: Beautiful praying Madonna in soft pastel shades has an exquisite face. Marked Inarco, Japan, E166/L. (7½")

Middle: Madonna with child is done in earth tones and ornamented with gold. No marks. (6¾")

Right: Sweet-faced Madonna in pastel shades has her arms crossed. Marked Dickson, made in Japan. (7½")

Left: All white praying Madonna has a gentle face. Marked Inarco, Cleve, Ohio, Japan, E-322. (6″)

Middle: Modest nun in black habit and white wimple has her hands folded in prayer. She is wearing a painted-gold cross. Marked Velco, Japan, 3809. (6½″)

Right: White Madonna wearing a halo is decorated with gold. No marks. (6½″)

Dreamy lady with light brown hair rests her chin on entwined fingers. Her outfit includes a pale pink dress, pearl jewelry and three roses tucked in her hair. Marked Inarco, © 1961, E-534. (7″)

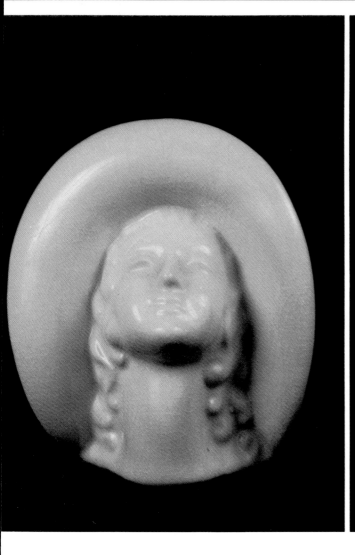

All white lady, wearing a wide brimmed hat, is looking upward. She could be used as a wall pocket or vase. Marked U.S.A. (5¼″)

Humorous white kitten holding two blue flowers has a pink nose and eyelids. Hard to find. Marked Napco-ware, C-7439. (5¾″)

Alluring lady with upswept black hair is wearing a white hat and gown garnished with rhinestones. No marks. (7¼")

Left: Young child with yellow flowers in her upswept brown hair is wearing a yellow dress. Marked Wales, made in Japan. (5¾")

Middle: Demure, black-haired belle is wearing a large pink hat and a matching dress adorned with a gold bow. No marks. (7½")

Right: Young girl with downcast eyes has blue flowers ornamenting her brown hair. She wears a pink dress with puffed sleeves and white collar. Marked Wales, made in Japan. (5¾")

Left: Good-looking miss with downcast eyes is wearing a yellow hat with black ribbon and a black dress with white collar and gold buckle. No marks. (4½")

Middle: Lady with a strange mixture of blonde and black hair is wearing a white glove, pearl jewelry, a blue dress with white collar, a gold flower brooch, and a white hat. Marked Bradley Exclusive, Japan. (6½")

Right: Lovely, brown-haired woman with uplifted hand and downcast eyes is wearing a dark green gown, pearl jewelry, and a green hat trimmed in white and gold. Marked Dickson, made in Japan. (4½")

Three enchanting oriental beauties are wearing ornate white and gold headgear. Two are holding fans in their uplifted hands. All three are marked Irice, made in Japan. They were probably sold holding either bath salts or sachet. (4½", 4½", 4")

Left: This proud, brown haired lady is ready for a festive party in a blue evening gown, earrings, and elaborate pink hairbow. No marks. (5½")
Middle: Lady with short brown hair and overdone eye-liner is wearing pearl jewelry, mustard yellow dress, and a black hat trimmed with a mustard yellow ribbon. Marked Rubens, Japan, 4106. (5")
Right: Attractive, musing lady with downcast eyes and tilted face is wearing a pearly white glove, dress, and hat trimmed in yellow. Marked 1843. (5¾")

Left: Wide-eyed lass with brown hair is wearing a fancy dress decorated with a red and white striped bow and a matching hat. No marks. (6¼")

Right: Adorable, little blonde girl with happy face is dressed for the winter holidays. She is wearing a red hat embellished with holly leaves, candy striped mittens, and a red coat trimmed in white fur fastened with a large gold button. Marked © Reliable Glassware and Pottery 1956, 3088. (6")

Left: Brown-haired woman is wearing a ring on her uplifted hand. She is garbed in a blue frock with white collar, pearl earrings, and black hat with white ribbon and gold buckle. Marked Japan. (5½")

Middle: Pleasant faced damsel has her brown hair brushed to one side. She is wearing a pink dress with a small blue print and a white Peter Pan collar, earrings, and pink hat trimmed with two flowers. Marked Napco, © 1960, Japan, C4554B. (6½")

Right: Dignified lady, glancing to her right, is arrayed in a white hat garnished with gold, pearl earrings, painted on pearl necklace, and a white dress with gold print and dark green collar. Marked Napco, © 1956, Japan, C2638c. (6")

Left: Black haired lady, with one shoulder raised, has a yellow rosebud tucked in the bodice of her purple dress. She is also wearing a pink and red flower in her hair, yellow flower earrings, and a white and yellow hat. Marked Made in Japan. (4½")

Middle: Long haired lady with downcast eyes is dressed like a southern belle in a red dress and large blue garden party hat trimmed in red with purple flowers. Marked Napco, © 1959, Japan, C3812B. (6")

Right: Restrained lady with brown hair is modestly attired in a pink dress, earrings, and pink hat with white and gold band. Marked Napco, © 1960, Japan, C48976. (5")

Left: Attractive, brown-haired lady is wearing a black dress trimmed in white. Her hat is edged with black and sports a large blue bow. Marked Relpo, Chicago, Ill, made in Japan, K1836. (7″)

Middle: Pretty blonde lady has her white-gloved hand touching her chin. She is wearing blue earrings, a blue glass jewel necklace, pink dress, and pink straw hat decorated with a bow. Marked Relpo, Chicago, Ill, made in Japan, A-1558. (5½″)

Right: Lady with a white and gold flower in her short brown hair is wearing pearl earrings, fancy pearl and gold chain necklace, and a simple black dress. Marked Inarco, E-2104. (7″)

Left: Pretty blonde with downcast eyes and tilted face is wearing a black dress edged in gold and ornamented with two pink roses. Marked Japan. (5")

Middle: Black haired lady with lustre finish is wearing a wide brimmed pink hat and a pink dress decorated with white and gold. Marked Stanfordware, Sterling, Ohio. (7")

Right: Dainty lady with black hair touched with gold is wearing a green gown, gold jewelry, and a green hat trimmed with white and gold flowers. No marks. (4¾")

Many of the Lady Head Vases produced came in more than one size. The three vases shown are marked Napcoware. (4½", 5¾", 3¾")

Left: Delicate lady has her blonde hair adorned with two white and gold flowers. She is wearing pearl earrings and a black dress decorated with a white and gold bow. Marked Enesco, Japan. (4½")

Middle: Handsome woman with blonde hair streaked with white is rigged out in a pink dress edged in maroon, black glove, and a white cravat dotted with gold. Marked Japan. (5½")

Right: Brown-haired damsel is clad in a mustard yellow dress printed with white flowers. Marked Royal Crown, Handpainted 3066. (4½")

Left: Aristocratic, black haired lady is arrayed in a white and gold dress, veil and tiara. Marked Stanfordware, Sterling, Ohio. (6½")
Right: White and gold rustic miss with braided hair is wearing a pink dress trimmed in gold and matching hat decorated with yellow roses. No marks. (6¼")

Left: Shy looking lady with a white bow in her brown hair is wearing a black dress with white collar and a heart-shaped, gold and black brooch. No marks. (5½")

Middle: Charming maiden with her brown hair tied with bows is attired in a sailor dress with a white collar piped with red. Marked Brinn's, Pittsburg, Pa., made in Japan. (5 ½")

Right: Modish woman with her brown hair fixed in long bangs and soft curls tied with a blue ribbon is wearing a turtleneck dress and blue earrings. Marked Caffco, Japan, E-31-5. (5½")

Left: Blasé blonde is wearing pearl jewelry and a black dress decorated with white sequins. Marked Caffco, Japan, E3284. (7½")
Right: Enchanting lady with her long curly hair tied with a large pink bow is wearing pearl earrings and a blue and white dress. Marked Enesco, Japan. (6¾")

Left: Little girl with brown hair is wearing a high collared green dress and a flat purple and black hat. Her hand is holding the base for an umbrella which is missing. Marked Japan. (5½")

Middle: Comely lady with downcast eyes and reddish brown hair is wearing a plain black dress. Marked Inapco, E3412. (5¾")

Right: Demure damsel with brown hair is wearing a green dress with puffed sleeves. Her two hands are touching. No marks. (5¾")

Left: Smiling adolescent with yellow hair is wearing white gloves on her hands, blue dress, and a blue hat trimmed with yellow flowers and a white and red striped bow. No marks. (3")

Right: Winsome young maiden with light brown hair looks like she is singing. Her outfit includes a blue and white striped gown and a blue hat edged in gold and white. No marks. (4¾")

Left: Handsome miss with brown hair, tilted face, and downcast eyes is wearing a white dress. Marked MS, 606B, Japan. (5¾")

Middle: Pretty blonde is wearing pearl ear studs and a black dress trimmed with white sequins. Marked Royal-crown, Handpainted, 3666. (4½")

Right: Beguiling black girl with downcast eyes and slightly parted lips is very rare. She is attired in a dark mustard yellow dress and a matching hair bow. Marked 50/423. (5½")

101

Left: Attractive lady with brown hair is wearing a green gown decorated with white ruffles edged in gold, with black buttons and bow. Marked E3285. (7")

Middle: Lady head lipstick holder is arrayed in a red dress. A ribbon ornamented with daisies decorates her hair. No marks. (6½")

Right: Lovely lass with long brown hair is wearing pearl earrings, yellow dress with white collars, and a matching yellow hairbow. Marked C8494. (7")

Three refined ladies with their white faces and hair decorated with gold were used by Irice (Irving W. Rice Co. of New York) to hold flower sachet. (4¼", 4¼", 4¼")

Left: Lady with white hair garnished with gold is wearing a pale green dress edged in gold and a matching hat trimmed with a pink rose. No marks. (6½")

Middle: Lady with gold eyelashes and white hair touch with gold is wearing a grass green dress trimmed in white and matching hat ornamented with a pink rose. No marks. (5¼")

Right: Pretty lady with her white face and hair trimmed with gold is wearing a yellow dress embellished with a pink rosebud and a matching hat. No marks. (6½")

Left: Genteel blonde with her chin resting on her hand is wearing a black dress with white and gold cuff, matching hat, and pearl jewelry. Marked Inarco, © 1961, E-190/5. (5")

Middle: Blasé lady with short, light brown hair is wearing pearl jewelry, white turtleneck sweater, black jacket, and black hair ribbon. Marked Napco-ware, Japan, C8497. (7")

Right: Beautiful woman with streaked hair is looking over her shoulder. She is wearing pearl earrings, black dress, and a white, gold, and pearl brooch. Marked Napcoware, Japan, C7471. (4¾")

PRICE GUIDE

Page 9: left-15; right-20
Page 10: left-12.50; middle-12.50; right-12.50
Page 11: left-12.50; middle-10.00; right-12.50
Page 12: left-12.50; middle-12.50; right-12.50
Page 13: left-12.50; middle-12.50; right-12.50
Page 14: left-15.00; middle-18.00; right-12.50
Page 15: left-12.50; middle-12.50; right-12.50
Page 16: left-12.50; middle-12.50; right-12.50
Page 17: left-12.50; middle-12.50; right-12.50

Page 18: left-18.00; right-18.00
Page 19: left-10.00; middle-10.00; right-12.50
Page 20: left-12.50; middle-15.00; right-12.50
Page 21: left-12.50; middle-12.50; right-12.50
Page 22: left-15.00; middle-12.50; right-12.50
Page 23: left-12.50; middle-12.50; right-12.50
Page 24: left-12.50; middle-15.00; right-12.50
Page 25: left-22.00; middle-12.50; right-25.00
Page 26: left-12.50; middle-15.00; right-12.50

Page 27: left-12.50; middle-15.00; right-12.50

Page 28: left-12.50; middle-15.00; right-12.50

Page 29: left-12.50; middle-12.50; right-15.00

Page 30: left-12.50; middle-15.00; right-12.50

Page 31: left-12.50; right-20.00

Page 32: left-20.00; right-20.00

Page 33: left-12.50; middle-25.00; right-12.50

Page 34: left-12.50; middle-12.50; right-12.50

Page 35: left-12.50; middle-12.50; right-12.50

Page 36: left-12.50; middle-15.00; right-12.50

Page 37: left-12.50; middle-12.50; right-15.00

Page 38: left-17.50; middle-17.50; right-17.50

Page 39: left-20.00; middle-20.00; right-20.00

Page 40: left-17.50; middle-17.50; right-17.50

Page 41: top left-25.00; top middle-17.50; top right-20.00
bottom left-12.50; bottom middle-12.50; bottom right-12.50

Page 42: left-20.00; middle-20.00; right-20.00

Page 43: left-12.50; middle-12.50; right-12.50

Page 44: left-15.00; middle-15.00; right-15.00

Page 45: left-15.00; middle-15.00; right-15.00

Page 46: top left-25.00; top middle-25.00; top right-25.00
bottom left-12.50; bottom middle-12.50; bottom right-12.50

Page 47: left-15.00; middle-17.50; right-12.50

Page 48: left-12.50; middle-15.00; right-12.50

Page 49: left-12.50; middle-15.00; right-12.50

Page 50: left-12.50; middle-15.00; right-12.50

Page 51: left-12.50; middle-12.50; right-12.50

Page 52: left-15.00; middle-15.00; right-15.00

Page 53: left-12.50; middle-12.50; right-12.50

Page 54: left-12.50; middle-12.50; right-12.50

Page 55: left-17.50; middle-12.50; right-17.50

Page 56: left-12.50; middle-12.50; right-12.50

Page 57: left-12.50; middle-12.50; right-12.50

Page 58: left-12.50; right-25.00

Page 59: left-12.50; middle-12.50; right-12.50

Page 60: left-15.00; right-25.00

Page 61: left-12.50; middle-20.00; right-12.50

Page 62: left-12.50; middle-12.50; right-10.00

Page 63: left-12.50; middle-12.50; right-12.50

Page 64: left-12.50; middle-12.50; right-12.50

Page 65: left-12.50; middle-17.50; right-12.50

Page 66: left-20.00; right-17.50

Page 67: left-12.50; middle-12.50; right-12.50

Page 68: left-12.50; middle-12.50; right-12.50

Page 69: left-12.50; middle-10.00; right-12.50

Page 70: left-12.50; middle-12.50; right-12.50

Page 71: left-12.50; middle-12.50; right-12.50

Page 72: left-15.00; middle-15.00;

right-15.00
Page 73: left-10.00; right-12.50
Page 74: left-12.50; right-12.50
Page 75: left-15.00; middle-15.00; right-15.00
Page 76: left-12.50; right-35.00
Page 77: left-12.50; middle-12.50; right-12.50
Page 78: left-17.50; middle-12.50; right-17.50
Page 79: left-12.50; middle-12.50; right-12.50
Page 80: left-7.50; middle-7.50; right-7.50
Page 81: left-7.50; right-7.50
Page 82: left-20.00; middle-20.00; right-20.00
Page 83: left-17.50; middle-17.50; right-20.00
Page 84: 15.00
Page 85: left-17.50; right-8.00
Page 86: 16.00
Page 87: left-12.50; middle-15.00;

right-12.50
Page 88: left-12.50; middle-12.50; right-12.50
Page 89: top left-20.00; top middle-20.00; top right-20.00
bottom left-12.50; bottom middle-12.50; bottom right-12.50
Page 90: left-15.00; right-17.00
Page 91: top left-12.50; top middle-12.50; top right-12.50
bottom left-12.50; bottom middle-12.50; bottom right-12.50
Page 92: left-15.00; middle-12.50; right-15.00
Page 93: left-12.50; middle-17.50; right-12.50
Page 94. left-10.00; middle-12.50; right-10.00
Page 95: left-12.50; middle-12.50; right-12.50
Page 96: left-20.00; right-15.00

Page 97: left-12.50; middle-12.50; right-12.50
Page 98: left-15.00; right-15.00
Page 99: left-8.00; middle-12.50; right-12.50
Page 100: left-12.50; right-15.00
Page 101: left-12.50; middle-12.50; right-25.00
Page 102: top left-15.00; top middle-17.50; top right-15.00
bottom left-10.00; bottom middle-15.00; bottom right-10.00
Page 103: left-12.50; middle-12.50; right-12.50
Page 104: left-12.50; middle-15.00; right-12.50
Back cover: 20.00